Protect Our Planet

Polluted Air

Angela Royston

Heinemann Library
Chicago, IL

© 2008 Heinemann Library
a division of Reed Elsevier Inc.

Customer Service **888-454-2279**

Design: Joanna Hinton-Malivoire
Picture research: Melissa Allison, Fiona Orbell and Erica Martin
Production: Duncan Gilbert
Printed and bound in China by South China Printing Co. Ltd.

12 11 10 09 08
10 9 8 7 6 5 4 3 2 1

10-digit ISBN: 1-4329-0925-8 (hc)
                 1-4329-0931-2 (pb)

Library of Congress Cataloging-in-Publication Data

Royston, Angela.
  Polluted air / Angela Royston.
     p. cm. -- (Protect our planet)
  Includes bibliographical references and index.
  ISBN 978-1-4329-0925-3 (hc) -- ISBN 978-1-4329-0931-4 (pb) 1. Air--Pollution--Juvenile literature. 2. Atmosphere--Juvenile literature. I. Title.
  TD883.13.R69 2008
  628.5'3--dc22
                              2007043914

Acknowledgements
The publishers would like to thank the following for permission to reproduce photographs: © Alamy pp.**16** (David Robertson, **11** (moodboard), **23** (Paul Glendell), **20** (Philip Bigg), **12** (Tom Uhlman); © Corbis pp.**22**, **25** (Abode, Beateworks), **27** (Andrew Fox), **7** (moodboard), **24** (Paulo Fridman), **26** (Roger Ressmeyer); © Ecoscene pp.**17** (Erik Schaffer), **6** (Fritz Polking); © Getty Images p.**13** (Photodisc); © Panos pp.**15** (Dermot Tatlow), **29** (Mark Henley), **10** (Simon Horton); © Pearson Education Ltd p.**19** (David Rigg); © Photolibrary pp.**14**(Japack Photo Library), **5** (Nordicphotos), **28** (Rob Cousins), **21** (Schmuel Thaler); © Science Photo Library p.**4** (Tom Van Sant, Geosphere Project, Santa Monica); © Still Pictures p.**8** (F.Herrmann).

Cover photograph of traffic in winter reproduced with permission of © Masterfile (Gary Gerovac).

Contents

Some words are shown in bold, **like this**. You can find out what they mean by looking in the Glossary.

What Is Air?

Air is a mixture of gases that surrounds our planet, the Earth. You cannot see the air, but you can feel it when you run and when you fly a kite.

The thin band of air around the Earth is shown in bright blue.

Clouds are made of tiny drops of water in the air. The air stretches for several miles above the clouds. The air becomes thinner the higher it is above the ground.

Why Is Air Important?

Oxygen is one of the gases in the air. Living things need oxygen to stay alive. Animals breathe in oxygen to get the energy they need to move around.

The faster an animal runs, the more oxygen it needs to breathe in.

Carbon dioxide is another gas that is in the air. Humans and other animals breathe out carbon dioxide.

Where Does Oxygen Come From?

Plants make **oxygen** when they create plant food. Their leaves take in **carbon dioxide** from the air. They use sunlight to change carbon dioxide and water into plant food.

Leaves make plant food.

When plants make plant food, they also make oxygen. The oxygen escapes into the air. This creates more oxygen for animals to breathe in.

Plants use water, sunlight, and carbon dioxide from the air to make plant food.

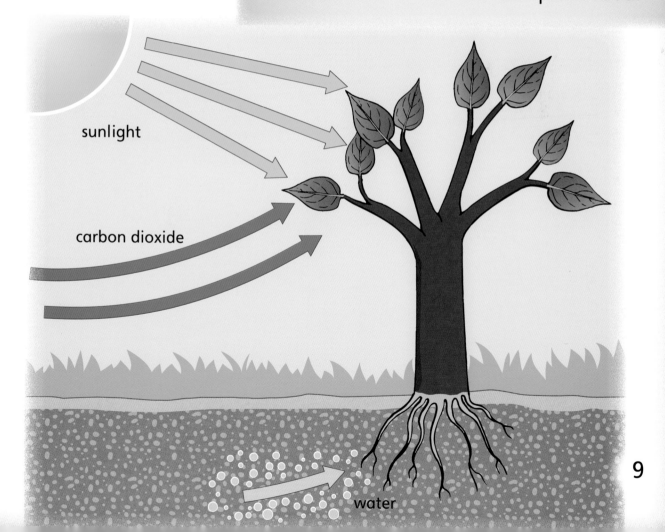

sunlight

carbon dioxide

water

9

What Is Air Pollution?

Dirt or other harmful things in the air is called air **pollution**. The air in cities is usually more **polluted** than in the country. Most pollution is caused by vehicles, factories, and **power stations**.

Some big cities have a cloud of pollution hanging over them.

This boy is taking medicine for asthma.

If the air is very dirty, people can become sick. They may also have trouble breathing. **Asthma** is an illness that makes it difficult to breathe. People with asthma may have an asthma attack when the air is very polluted.

How Do Vehicles Pollute the Air?

Airplanes, cars, trucks, and other vehicles have engines that burn **fuel** to make them work. Almost all fuel is made from **oil**. As vehicles burn fuel, they create **waste** gases.

Cars release waste gases into the air.

The waste gases escape into the air. The gases mix with the air and **pollute** it. Waste gases include **carbon dioxide** and several poisonous gases.

What Else Causes Air Pollution?

Most factories and **power stations** cause air **pollution**. Factories make many kinds of things. For example, toys, clothes, cars, and even some foods are made in factories. Many factories create **waste chemicals** that **pollute** the air.

The air pollution shown here comes from a factory.

The coal used by power stations has to be brought up from under the ground.

Power stations make **electricity**. We use electricity to light our rooms and to run televisions, computers, and other machines. Most power stations burn **fuels** such as coal or **oil** to make electricity. Burning coal and oil makes waste gases that pollute the air.

Polluted Rain

Waste gases from factories and **power stations** rise up into the air. The gases mix with drops of water that form in clouds. This causes **polluted** rain. Sometimes rain also contains **soot** and other pieces of dirt.

Half of this building has been cleaned. The other half is still black from soot and dirt in the rain.

Acid rain has eaten away some of the carving on this wall.

Polluted rain is called **acid rain**. Acid rain damages buildings. It can also kill trees. When acid rain flows into lakes, it can kill fish and other animals.

The Ozone Layer

The **ozone layer** is a layer of ozone gas that is high above the clouds. The ozone layer protects us from the harmful rays of the Sun.

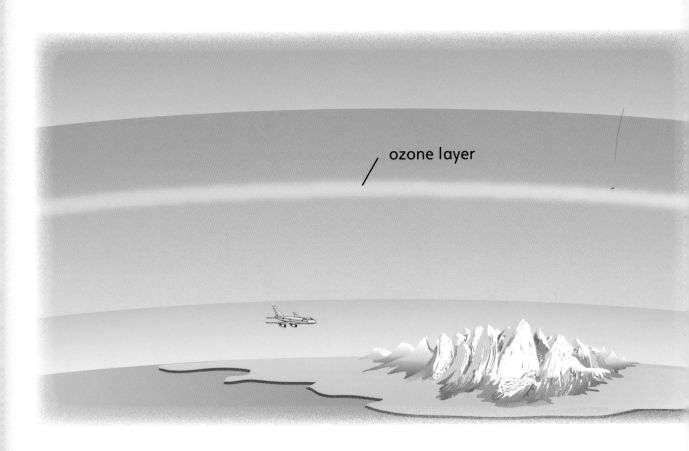

ozone layer

Some of the **chemicals** that are used to make refrigerators work can damage the ozone layer.

Some air **pollution** destroys some of the ozone in the ozone layer. When ozone is destroyed, the ozone layer becomes thinner. Then it does not protect us as well from the Sun.

Cleaner Cars

Scientists are finding new ways to reduce air **pollution**. They are making vehicles that make less pollution. Some vehicles run on **natural gas**. Natural gas makes less pollution than gasoline made from oil.

This taxi runs on natural gas.

These cars use electric motors.

Other vehicles use an **electric motor** that does not need gasoline. **Hybrid** cars use an electric motor and a small gasoline engine. They create less pollution than regular cars.

Clean Ways of Making Electricity

New kinds of **power stations** are being built that make less **pollution**. They use sunlight, the wind, or running water to make **electricity**.

These panels use sunlight to make electricity.

wind turbine

People can make their own electricity without making pollution. A small **wind turbine** on the roof of a building can make enough electricity to run the lights and computers inside.

Cleaner Factories

Some factories are becoming cleaner. They make less air **pollution** by trapping the dirt and **waste** gases before they reach the air.

This factory makes a small amount of air pollution.

The hood over this stove is a filter that cleans the air.

Factories trap dirt by **filtering** the waste gases. A filter works like a coffee filter. It traps things that are too big to pass through it.

Getting Rid of Trash

People who live in the United States create a lot of trash. When trash is burned, it **pollutes** the air. Some of the gases are poisonous.

All of this trash is being taken to be burned.

Plastic, paper, metal, and glass can
be collected for recycling.

One way to reduce air **pollution** is to make
less trash. People can do this by buying
things that do not have much packaging.
They can also help by **recycling** as much
trash as possible.

Avoiding Air Pollution

There are several things you can do to avoid breathing in air **pollution**. When you walk or ride a bike, try to avoid busy roads. Keep to small roads and back streets.

In some places, special paths are made for cyclists to use. These help them keep away from busy roads.

In very **polluted** places, people wear face masks so that they do not breathe in polluted air.

Some countries are working to limit the amount of pollution they create. They set limits for how much pollution factories and **power stations** can create. The more people work together to reduce air pollution, the cleaner our air will be.

Glossary

acid rain rain that kills leaves and eats away at buildings

asthma illness that can make it difficult to breathe

carbon dioxide one of the gases in the air

chemical substance that things are made of

electricity form of energy used to make machines work

electric motor engine that uses electricity to make something work

filtering using a fine mesh to separate solids, such as dust, from a liquid or gas

fuel substance such as gas, wood, or coal that is burned to give heat, light, or power

hybrid mixture of two or more things

natural gas gas that burns easily and is used for fuel

oil liquid that burns easily and is used for fuel

oxygen one of the gases in the air

ozone layer layer of ozone gas that protects us from the Sun's rays

pollute make dirty

pollution dirt or waste gases or chemicals

power station building where electricity is made

recycling processing used materials so that they can be used again

soot black dust made when coal and other things are burned

waste things that are thrown out because they are not wanted any more

wind turbine machine that makes electricity using blades that spin in the wind

Find Out More

Books to Read

Smith, Viv. *I Can Help Clean Our Air*. New York: Franklin Watts Ltd, 2001.

Fix, Alexandra. *Plastic*. Chicago: Heinemann Library, 2007.

Websites

www.epa.gov/kids/air.htm
This website tells you about air pollution and what you can do to help keep the air clean.

Index